MW00930598

ROOFING 101: A COMPLETE GUIDE TO ROOFING

The Ultimate Homeowner and Handyman
Guide To Understanding Roofing Types and
Installation Tips

By Anthony Legins

Copyright © 2021

Disclaimer

Contents

Roofing Basics

Roofing is something that every homeowner should be familiar with; after all, it is the roof that protects you from the elements and is directly related to your home's quality of life.

The research for materials and negotiations with professionals can be tiring, and even before any supplies are purchased or construction begins, you may find yourself giving up the idea due to the sheer scope of the project and everything it entails.

If you want a new roof for your home, you'll need to consider how you'll get the job done.

Many people believe they can do the work themselves only to discover later that they can't, leaving them in a desperate situation that necessitates immediate assistance, which usually costs much more than if they had planned things properly.

If you're thinking about getting a new roof for your home, you won't want to handle it alone. Not only is the construction dangerous, but it is hard to select the correct roofing materials and to construct it in a structurally reliable manner.

Of course, there are benefits to hiring a professional to install your roofing.

The most significant benefit of hiring a roofing contractor is that you will be able to receive expert advice on the materials you require, both for aesthetic and practical reasons.

You will be able to chat with your roofing contractor if you have any questions concerning roof damage or anything to do with style.

Another benefit of hiring a roofing contractor is that you can rest assured that the job will be done correctly the first time. The roofing contractor's work should be as efficient as possible, allowing you to spend the least amount of time on your property and causing the least amount of discomfort for you and your family while the work is being done.

Your roofing contractor may not only be able to do what you need, but he or she may also be able to see any potential issue areas.

This is essential because if you can get these areas repaired as soon as possible, you may be able to save a lot of damage to your property later.

Because most people do not replace their roof every few years, it is critical to have a roofing job done correctly and completely. You should consider all facets of this project before signing any contracts or purchasing any materials.

Naturally, you'll want to check to see if the contractor you're considering hiring is the right person for the job, so ask for references.

The easiest way to do this is to inquire about other properties in your community that they have worked on, inspect the work, and listen to other people's experiences, which will help you make a more informed decision.

This way, you can drive by and look at the roof and ask the people what they thought of the kind of service they received.

You will be able to prevent running into problems after they have already started the task if you check out possible contractors ahead of time.

Using a Certified Roofing Contractor

The importance of a sound roof

Your home is built to keep you, your family, and your belongings safe from the elements, and the roof is the section of the house that receives the most abuse while performing this vital function.

Despite this, it is the one feature of the home that people wanting to buy a home, as well as those looking to repair or maintain their current home, overlook the most. However, without proper maintenance and frequent care, your roof is prone to leaks and can easily be damaged in the worst of weather.

The annual maintenance of your roof

Checking your roof on an annual basis should become a habit, and if you don't feel confident enough to know where to look, hire an expert to do it for you.

Using a qualified roofing contractor ensures that you are dealing with an expert who knows what to look for and can provide you with the best advise if any work is required.

The constant pounding of the sun, rain, wind, hail, snow, and ice formation puts pressure on any material or substance, and your roof is no exception.

A licensed roofing contractor can tell you if you have appropriate protection in place to guarantee that your roof continues to do its job.

Going up on the roof yourself

When microscopic fractures occur in a roof, a leak may not be noticeable right quickly, and the water can often travel away to sections you can't see.

You might not be able to see these minor areas of damage without getting up on the roof yourself and trying to climb on the roof yourself isn't everyone's idea of a pleasant Saturday afternoon.

To avoid damage to your roof and possible personal injury, you should hire the services of a licensed roofing contractor.

A qualified roofing contractor

A licensed roofing contractor has the skills and qualifications to execute any project, from certifying your roof (typically for two years, during which time they are liable for repairs) to totally taking down and replacing your old roof with a new and more effective one.

A professional roofing contractor can advise you on the best tools, materials, and systems to utilize to provide your home with the protection it requires.

Finding a certified roofing contractor

You have various alternatives when it comes to finding a professional roofing contractor. Ask family and friends if they have used the services of a good certified roofing contractor.

However, you should never take someone's word for anything without first conducting your own investigation.

Request a list of people who are registered roofing contractors from the people in charge of issuing licenses in your state.

Before contacting them in this manner, you'll have already verified their license.

Tips For Hiring A Reputable Roofing Contractor

Shingles that are curling or cracked. There are ceiling leaks. In the gutters, there are far too many asphalt granules. Any of these warning signals could indicate that it's time to replace your roof.

So, where should you begin? With the help of a dependable contractor.

Schedule a meeting with three or more of the roofers you've been recommended and ask them the following questions:

- **What is the company's full name and address?** This will confirm the company's legitimacy.

- **Is the business covered by insurance?** Contractors should carry both general liability and workers' compensation insurance to protect you as the homeowner in the event of an accident.

- **Is the company a certified or licensed contractor?** Although licensure is not required in all areas, it is a positive indication that the contractor is knowledgeable and competent.

- **How long has the company been in operation?** The longer a company has been in operation, the better; most small businesses have a three-year lifespan.

- **Will the company provide previous job references or referrals?** Request a list of former employers' names and phone numbers, as well as pics of the roofer's completed work.

- **What is the warranty on the company's workmanship?** Warranties covering the work of the installer should normally last at least one year.

- **What is the company's track record when it comes to resolving customer issues?** Request a referral from an customer where they had to deal with a complaint. This will demonstrate to the homeowner how the contractor deals with issues when they happen.

Different Types of Roofing Materials

Various types of roofing materials are currently available on the market.

The location, local weather conditions, aesthetic value, and budget are the major elements to keep in mind when choosing the appropriate one for your home.

Although every nook and cranny should be thoroughly considered when creating your own home, the roof should be given top priority. So, to assist you in your search for the ideal roof, here are the various types of roofing materials currently in use.

In the United States, asphalt shingles are the most popular roofing material.

Asphalt shingles have a high volume of manufacture and a low application cost, making it difficult for other types of roofing materials to compete.

Homeowners will have a better chance of finding one that suits their style and preferences because they are available in a variety of colors and designs.

The ongoing requirement for maintenance and frequent checkups to monitor damaged shingles that need replacement is one of the main disadvantages of asphalt shingles.

It's also a good idea to avoid painting asphalt shingles because this would speed up the deteriorating process.

Another option for roofing materials is metal.

This material is commonly utilized in commercial projects, but some homeowners have chosen it for its longevity, durability, and aesthetic appeal.

Metal roofing goods are divided into two categories: panels and shingles.

Metal shingles are made to look like wood shakes, tiles, and shingles, which are common roof coverings.

Because metal roofs are excellent insulators, they are known to drastically lower energy bills. The disadvantage of employing metal roofing materials is that they are prone to denting.

Slate is considered shatterproof; however it is usually more expensive than the other types of roofing materials currently available.

Slate roofs are generally meant to be lightweight and resistant to adverse weather, and most come with a 50-year warranty.

Your home would benefit greatly from tile roofing. They are normally built of clay, slate, or concrete and are available in a variety of forms and sizes.

Tiles are the only roofing materials that come with a lifetime warranty among the many types of roofing materials.

Tile roofs are so tough that they can withstand extreme temperatures and earthquakes. The entire weight of your roof might be fairly hefty because it is constructed of a solid material.

To support the additional load, you'd need some structural reinforcements. There are, however, lighter substitutes that look and perform similarly to the genuine thing.

With so many options available today, it would be wise to spend some time researching the best roofing material for your needs.

This isn't a minor consideration because you'll be living under that roof for the better part of your life.

Classic Roofing

With so many roofing styles and designs to pick from on the market today, you'll probably need some assistance to steer you in the right direction.

Choosing the appropriate roofing design for your home requires careful preparation and a significant amount of time. Roofs, after all, play a significant role in the overall appearance of your property.

When it comes to classic roofing styles, the possibilities are practically endless. You can choose from a variety of styles, ranging from clay to metal tile, to complement your property.

Classic roofing sometimes necessitates a high level of skill and craftsmanship. Adding roof embellishments would substantially enhance the roof's beauty and elegance.

That is why, in addition to selecting high-quality materials, it is critical to hire only the best roofing contractors in your area.

This will ensure high-quality work and your complete pleasure.

People nowadays choose roofs that are almost maintenance-free. Wooden shakes, on the other hand, would require extra attention and protection.

However, there are a dozen alternatives to the classic roofing often found in archetypal homes.

Frequently, recycled roofing materials are completely suitable for assisting you in creating the classic roofing design you desire. If you like a traditional, classic roofing design, lightweight, synthetic materials are also recommended.

Synthetic roofing materials can frequently endure high winds and other severe weather conditions better than traditional roofing materials.

Steel tiles are designed to look like traditional roofing tiles, but with the added benefit of being easier to install and far less expensive.

Synthetic roofing materials come in a variety of styles and textures, allowing you to get the look you want for your roof.

Not only will the synthetic classic roofing provide you with protection and coverage against adverse weather conditions, but you can also anticipate it to last longer than traditional cedar or slate roofs.

Many contemporary slates and imitation shakes are packed with rubber compounds, making them more durable and fire resistant while also better inhibiting damaging UV radiation. Air-pressured nail guns make it much easier to install synthetic materials.

When determining which roofing type to use, make sure to weigh the advantages of each option.

Choose a style that will complement the beauty of your home while also providing the durability you need.

Roofing Underlayment

Roofing underlayment is the second layer of protection that a roofing system requires. It protects the roof from moisture and other elements that can shorten the life of the roof.

A increasing number of homeowners are aware of the importance of choosing the correct roofing underlayment for their roof. Felt, synthetics, and self-adhering ice-and-water barriers are the three types of underlayment available in the market today for homeowners to choose from.

However, when choosing the proper material for underlayment, keep the following aspects in mind.

In the event of a fire, a good material must be fire resistant, safeguarding the roofing system and the entire building. It should be able to endure the ferocity of heavy winds that could lift it and break it apart.

The underlayment material should be tough enough to resist tearing. Possible leaks are avoided in this instance.

Finally, it should be able to withstand a hard downpour.

Underlayment may appear to be an additional cost to the home, but it could save you money in the long run by protecting your property for a longer period of time.

Felt paper, or simply felt, is a material formed of paper that has been soaked in asphalt. It has been in use for more than five decades since it is simple to install and inexpensive.

However, one disadvantage of felt is that it is readily torn, especially in hot weather. Because the material is not porous, it tends to retain moisture and can be difficult to install due to its slick appearance, which can be difficult for the installer.

The most recent underlayment on the market is polypropylene-based. It serves the same purpose as second-degree protection for your roofing system against damaging factors.

Asphalt-saturated felt is less durable and lighter than synthetic underlayment. It is considerably safer to install than felt since it does not slip. The catch is that synthetic underlayment is far more expensive than felt, but it protects your roof better and lasts longer.

Polyester or fiberglass fabric is used in several synthetic underlayment.

The Self-adhering ice-and-water barrier is an underlayment that is primarily used to guard against ice and water.

The name implies that this underlayment may be installed without the need of fasteners, which eliminates the necessity for holes.

The trend started in New England, where the winters are harsh, and ice accumulates on rooftops. Because it conceals the punctures made by nails and staples in installing paper or synthetic underlayment, this underlayment can be used on top of felt or synthetics.

A good roofing underlayment is absolutely necessary for developing a long-lasting roofing system.

A wise investment in underlayment will help to protect both your property and your family.

Roofing Tools

Roofing tools are critical components in the roofing process. They make it simple and, in some cases, the only way to get started on your roofing project.

While learning the names and functions of each item isn't difficult, locating the tools and figuring out how to obtain them is.

The tools you wish to buy don't have to be expensive, but they should be long-lasting.

If you really want your roofing to be done correctly, you'll need to go out and find that tool.

The following is a list of high-performance hand tools you may need:
- Roofers Sheet Metal Tongs and Seamers
- Slate Hammers
- Slate Rippers
- Slate Cutters
- Molding Paint Scrapers
- Brick Hammers
- Brick Cutters
- Scribes
- Soldering Irons
- Tile Cutters
- Roofers Adze
- Roofers Axe

- Tinners Hammers
- Jointers
- Pointing Slickers
- Brick Chisels
- Masonry Chisels
- Boatswains Tools
- Wood Caulking Irons
- Riggers Tools
- Scaling Hammers
- Caulking Mallets
- Bale Hooks
- Gaffs, Draw Knives

Thor Roofing Layout Tape is a newly created product that helps carpenters install roofs. It has revolutionized the way roofs should be installed.

It has sped up roofing installation, reducing miscalculations to a bare minimum, allowing you to save more money.

The instrument is simple to use because it comes with an easy-to-follow tutorial, which is ideal for novices.

Thor roofing layout tape is guaranteed to be computer-adjustable, glare-free, and weatherproof.

Roofing tools are more than just an expense, they're an investment. Buying your own tools necessitates financial consideration.

So, before you go out and get a new one, look in your tool cabinet to see what you have. Because it's possible that you already have the tools you require.

Roofing Supplies

Building your own dream home is a fantastic achievement. Another is having it roofed tastefully and completely to your satisfaction.

Copper roofing material is preferred by people who want their roofs to seem classical with a touch of the Victorian Era.

Some people prefer clay roofing because they want to feel like they're in the countryside.

For those who want their roofs to have a vineyard or orchard feel, cedar shingle or slate is a preferable choice.

There are so many options, not to mention the other parts of a roofing system, that there may be even more.

In the market, there are numerous supplies from which to choose. These materials are supplied in a variety of home improvement stores that offer a variety of bundles to appeal to a wide range of market groups.

Roofing contractors can also provide valuable referrals to help you obtain the best value for your money.

Roofing material manufacturers are always developing their goods to provide the best solution to any roofing challenge.

They're going head-to-head in the roofing industry for the lion's share of the market. Because suppliers sometimes specialize their products and services to cater to their target market, not all of these items may be purchased from a single source.

Roofing materials can imply a variety of things to different individuals. But one thing should be clear: anything that has to do with roofing comes under this category.

Roofing supplies come in a wide variety of shapes and sizes. Roofing materials, such as metal, rubber, and cedar, which come in a variety of colors and shapes, are examples of roofing supplies.

This class could cover both simple and high-tech tools for installing roof systems.

Roofing supplies include sealants, coatings, several types of underlayment, and other insulating materials.

Cleaning products and other maintenance tools can be obtained in the roofing supplies area of your local home improvement store.

Whatever you require for your roof, whether it is a new roof, a replacement of an existing one, or anything that will be utilized to repair leaks or damaged areas, you must become familiar with the various roofing supplies.

A good visit to your local store can assist you in determining where to obtain the roofing material that you have always desired for your roof.

If you are fully informed about the various supplies sold in the roofing stores near you, you can make a sensible selection and the proper pick.

Roofing Nail Guns

Roofing nail guns are among the more severe DIY equipment, and they're typically only used by professionals.

If you're putting together a tiny chest of drawers or a bookcase, all you actually need is a regular hammer, but if you're building a roof on a two-story house, it could take weeks to nail a few nails in.

Roofing nail guns lighten the load and make the job go much faster and easier, so whether you're a novice or a pro, keep in mind that you won't get very far without them.

Why bother with roofing nail guns?

Roofing nail guns fire nails into wood or any other material for which they were designed, taking only a fraction of a second to 'hammer' in a single nail.

This eliminates the time and effort generally associated with pounding huge amounts of nails. They are highly handy, but if not handled properly, they may be rather deadly.

Spring loaded roofing nail guns

Spring-loaded roofing nail guns are the most basic and cost-effective nail guns available.

They use some really high tension springs to fire the nails out of the chamber and into the wood, and their ingenuity is fairly straightforward. Perhaps crude, but unquestionably effective!

These roofing nail guns still utilize a small amount of electric power to pull back the springs to the point where they can discharge at a fast enough rate to lodge into the wood.

Solenoid roofing nail guns

Electromagnetic polarization is used to power solenoid roofing nail guns. The polarization in the cannon reverses when you pull the trigger, repelling the nail away from the mechanism and into the wood.

This is a very important approach that is used in a variety of machines and tools and has been demonstrated to work for a long time.

There are very few parts that are likely to break, leaving you with powerless roofing nail guns; this durability is a significant advantage over the spring-loaded roofing nail guns, which wear out relatively quickly.

Pneumatic roofing nail guns

Compressed or pneumatic nail guns are the most common and commonly used form of roofing nail gun. A conventional air compressor can generate massive amounts of power by compressing air.

When you pull the trigger on a pneumatic roofing hammer drill, the pressure is utilized to hold the hammer in place so the nail isn't shot, but when you pull the trigger, it opens a tunnel that lets the compressed air out and dispels the nail quickly.

Because they simply require an air compressor to operate, these are the most popular roofing nail guns.

Air compressors can be powered in a variety of ways, and pneumatic roofing nail guns do not need to be plugged into the mains.

This saves money while also making it more reliable and convenient, not to mention safe when it starts to rain.

3-Tab Roofing Shingles

3-tab roofing shingles are characterized by three tabs or a length of three feet.

They are usually guaranteed for 20 years and contribute to the roof's smooth, defined appearance.

3-tab shingles are frequently available with limited warranties of 20, 25, or even 30 years, depending on the manufacturer.

They come in a range of colors, and it's also worth noting that 3-tab roofing shingles are among the most cost-effective shingles you can use on your house.

Are 3-Tab Roofing Shingles For You?

Check with your local homeowner's association before selecting on 3-tab roofing shingles for your property.

Some associations, in addition to having specific restrictions, do not allow the use of 3-tab shingles.

This may be true in locations where there is a lot of wind or other adverse weather, but double-check your local building codes to be sure.

Replacing 3-Tab Roofing Shingles

You have the option of replacing 3-tab roofing shingles yourself or hiring a professional roofing contractor.

Choose a warm, dry day if you opt to do the work yourself. If the roof is damp or slick, do not work on it.

Pry the tabs of the shingles upward, which overlap the damaged one, while you're on the roof.

Loosen the tabs and glue on the shingle's backside. Work carefully to prevent damaging the shingles next to you. On good shingles, if you raise too many tabs, they may crack.

For the shingle that you are removing, look for the nails holding it into place and remove them as well.

Remove any debris from the area where the old shingle was removed before installing the new shingle.

Locate the adhesive strips near the bottom of each of the three tabs with your new shingle in hand.

Install the new shingle by sliding it into place and securing it with nails.

The overlying tabs can be secured with roofing cement.

Contacting A Professional

Call a professional roofing contractor if you are unsure about working on your roof.

Shingled Roofing Installation

The first stage in shingle roofing installation is to draw lines to trace the shingle tops' alignment.

For nailing, these shingles will be positioned above the lines. The lines must be snapped from eave to peak across the roof.

Tracing the lines can be done with shingle bottoms or tapes, as manufacturers propose.

The shingles are now ready for installation after all the lay outing has been completed.

It's critical to space every other shingle by 6 inches to avoid leaking when they're overlapped, and to leave about 1/16 inch between each shingle.

Begin by nailing the first set of starter shingles in place, using four galvanized roofing nails per shingle. Then, starting with the drip edge suspended by 1/2 inch, start laying each shingle on top of the starter shingles.

Remember to nail each shingle from the bottom up next to the one before it, with a consistent nailing direction across the board.

This will prevent the roof from collapsing when shingled roofing is installed.

After the entire roof has been covered in shingles, the hip shingles are installed.

These will be installed on top of the ridge shingles, which are utilized to cover the roof planes' intersecting tops or peaks.

Trace a line across one side of the ridge with one hip shingle at each end.

Then start inserting additional all the way up to the ridge's center point, nailing them on both sides.

Applying the ridge shingles is the last phase in shingled roofing installation.

Unlike hip shingles, which are laid from one end to the other, ridge shingles are laid from one end to the other, with the highest wind direction in mind.

After that, fasten the last ridge shingle with two nails, which will be the only nails exposed after all the roofing work is finished.

Installing Rolled Roofing

Installing rolled roofing is a difficult task. When it comes to installing rolled roofing, there is no room for error, thus precision is essential.

After you've acquired your rolled roofing, don't forget to ask your suppliers for installation advice.

Check to see if the type you purchased requires special installation instructions, as installation is a one-time event that you can't undo.

However, the most basic advice for installing rolled roofing is to do so on a bright sunny day when the roofing material is at its most flexible.

Allow a day for the rolled roofing material to rest and flatten before laying it down for application. Curvy edges are avoided, and the material evens out the moisture in the sheet.

There are companies that sell easy-to-install roll roofing products. The idea is like that of ordinary household or office adhesive tape. You simply peel it off and place it in the appropriate location.

Make certain that the area where the rolled roofing will be installed is the correct size. This will let you cut the material without making any mistakes, reducing waste. However, before you can begin the installation, you must first clean the roof deck to provide an even and smooth surface. Be sure the surface is flat and smooth before you get started.

The assistance of professionals may be beneficial in achieving a better result when installing rolled roofing.

Metal Roofing

Metal is one of the most widely utilized roofing materials on the planet.

It is a popular choice among homeowners and builders because it is widely available in the market and comes in a variety of colors and styles.

Metal roofing is just as durable as other roofing materials, and while the initial cost is significant, the return on investment is also substantial.

At the end of the day, metal roofing will prove to be a cost-effective investment.

Metal roofing has drastically improved over the years, according to the Metal Roofing Alliance and the National Roofing Contractors Association in the United States.

It is lightweight, durable, and fire-resistant thanks to the utilization of cutting-edge technologies and novel materials.

There are many different types of metal roofing from which to choose. Galvanized steel, also known as GI sheets, is the most affordable option on the market and is quite popular among homeowners.

The Metal Roofing Alliance recommends using the G-90 type for roofing installation.

Metal roofing is low-maintenance and simple to keep clean. It can survive extreme weather and temperature fluctuations. Because of its conducting nature, it can easily draw heat, making it simple to melt snow throughout the winter. It is low-cost, leak-proof, and fire-resistant.

It is simple to set up because it may be installed over existing systems. Because of its recyclability, it is also environmentally friendly.

The roof will last for many more years, allowing you to recoup your investment.

Metal roofing will never go out of style since it adapts to changing needs for higher quality, lower cost, longer lifespan, and environmental friendliness.

Metal roofing will continue to be popular among consumers because it keeps up with the current trends and styles, which will appeal to the discerning and flawless tastes of the public.

Metal Roofing Materials

Metal roofing materials come in a variety of shapes and sizes. Some are shaped according to the buyer's specifications. Some are painted in bright hues, which add to the overall appeal of the structure.

Among metal roofing materials, aluminum is one of the most popular. It's small and light, making installation simple.

This metal can withstand a variety of standard weather conditions, allowing it to last as long as any other metal. However, in severe weather with strong gusty winds, this material may easily pull away.

Aluminum is one of the most cost-effective and easy-to-maintain materials.

Galvanized iron is another type of metal roofing material. This, like aluminum, is a lightweight substance. It offers a high level of corrosion and fire resistance.

Galvanized iron, also known as GI sheet, is a cost-effective option for a simple yet durable roofing system.

Copper is one of the oldest metal roofing materials, having been used for millennia.

Copper's dominance was questioned with the emergence of modern technologies. Its dominance over other roofing materials has decreased since today's homes and business owners desire a material that is as light as copper.

It's fascinating to notice that copper retains a sizable following. Copper roofs can still be found on old churches and on luxury mansions in high-end developments. It's because no other metal can produce the green patina appearance that copper can.

Copper is also an extremely durable metal. If properly maintained, it can last for more than 30 years.

Steel is one of the best metal roofing materials used by industrial plant owners, despite being as heavy as copper.

Steel is rarely used as a roof because of its considerable weight, which makes installation even more difficult.

Stainless steel metal roofs, in particular, are quite costly.

Corrugated or flat metal roofing materials are available. Some are made of slate, while others are made of shingles. Some are already coated and painted, while others remain unfinished.

Metal roofing is attractive and long-lasting, but proper care is required.

Metal Roofing: A Step-by-Step Guide

Have you considered installing a metal roof yourself? Don't give it a second thought.

Installing new metal roofing and even performing repairs is not as simple as you may believe. Learning how to install metal roofing is a difficult task.

It requires a variety of procedures and techniques, as well as the use of a variety of metal instruments and accessories.

Metal roofing is often installed by professionals because it is not an easy do-it-yourself project.

A competent roofing expert should be hired to build a moderate to complex metal roof.

Let's take a quick look at the procedures and standards for installing metal roofing.

The first step in learning how to install metal roofing is determining how much metal roofing is required, which can be done by measuring the roof's height, length, and edges.

If you're thinking of replacing your old roof, make sure to look for any loose roofing or damaged protrusions first.

Using a measuring square and a level, check the roof pitch and make a note of the manufacturer's minimal requirements.

The next step is to choose a roofing underlayment that will help prevent excessive moisture from building up on the metal roof during unfavorable weather conditions.

The underlayment must protrude 12 inches on all roof edges, expand 12 inches on vent pipes, and protrude 6 inches on sides.

If your metal roof is directly against the underlayment, it's advisable to use red rosin paper over the felt paper to prevent the metal from sticking to it.

The metal sheets will be the focus of the next few steps on how to install metal roofing. Bend each sheet against the building to easily reach and pull it up.

Use 14-inch metal wood screws every two feet on both sides to secure the metal roof to the wood slats. Then fold the first page over the second. Repeat with the rest of the roof until the final sheet is covered.

If there is any additional space past the edge, trim it with a tin snip before screwing in the final sheet.

5/16-inch lap screws are used to secure the metal sheets every four feet where two sheets overlap.

Begin by covering the borders of the roof with metal trim, as well as the roof ridge, which should be folded over to completely cover it.

For the metal trim, use 14-inch metal wood screws.

The next step is to install the closures, which are 3-foot foam rubber pieces. It will adhere itself to the opening along the edges since it has adhesive underneath.

These are merely the fundamentals of metal roofing installation. If you want to ask a professional, the process is much more complicated.

If you want to try your hand at roofing your garage, for example, make sure to follow the steps properly and use the proper tools.

Slate Roofing

Slate roofing is used by a number of households and commercial building owners for their roof projects. What is slate, exactly? Why would they chose a slate roof over a different sort of roof?

Slate is a quarried natural stone that is utilized for both interior and exterior applications.

Roofs, hallways, walls, fireplaces, pathways, roads, landscape elements, and more can all benefit from it.

This material is fireproof and lasts for hundreds of years, making it an excellent choice for rooftops and walls.

It is available in a variety of colors, including red, green, earth tones, gray-green, and other multi-colors.

The usage of slate for your rooftop enhances the elegance of your property, therefore it's worth considering.

Its vibrant appearance contributes to the building's charm. The hue of slate will vary depending on where it was mined and quarried. Slate shingles have been found to be extremely durable and hefty.

Because slate is handcrafted, its thickness, like that of a wood shingle, is not exact or consistent. Each slate may be 4 to 8 mm thick, but if the cut is less than 4 mm, it is likely to break.

Because slates are thick and heavy, the roofing structure's framework must be sturdy enough to support the weight of the slate roof tiles.

Natural slate can be found in around ten different states in the United States, all of which have quarries or mines where true slate can be obtained. However, as the expanding usage of slate as shingles and other goods slows due to its relatively high cost, these quarries are progressively disappearing.

Those who want to use slate roofing on their roof but can't afford to buy real slate might use synthetic slate roof shingles as an alternative.

Synthetic slate roofing is made from a blend of recycled rubber and plastic molded into the shape of real roof slates.

This is less expensive, lighter, and more durable than actual slate roofing since it is easier to transport and can be put with roof nails without worry of damaging the material. Because of its light weight, it may not be necessary for a roofing structure to have significant reinforcement to hold the roof tiles.

Its lifespan can be as long as a hundred years, just like a real slate roof.

If you're considering slate roofing for your roof, you now have the option of choosing between natural and synthetic slate.

Compare its features and benefits, as well as your financial constraints.

Architectural Roofing Shingles

Architects, builders, and homeowners have been on the lookout for versatile and affordable shingles that combine the aesthetic value of traditional roofing materials like cedar and shakes since the emergence of new roofing materials.

As a result of this demand, construction companies have developed a wide range of architectural roofing shingles.

Architectural roofing shingles are becoming increasingly popular among homeowners due to their superior appearance and enhanced longevity, all without the added cost of its original counterparts.

Architectural roofing shingles give your roof finish more character and offer a new dimension to the appearance of your property.

Take note of how houses with architectural roofing shingles stand out from the rest to properly appreciate the look. In most circumstances, these types of shingles are projected to provide stable shelter for 25 to 35 years.

The biggest disadvantage of architectural roofing shingles is that they are susceptible to algae and mildew, especially when wet leaves or debris accumulate on your roof.

If you reside in an area with a normally damp climate, copper-infused shingles are a good choice.

The random design of most architectural roofing shingles makes it far easier for roofers to lay than the regular 3-tab kind.

Traditional shingles must be properly aligned, or otherwise the roof would appear random and wavy.

Architectural roofing shingles, on the other hand, have a surface that hides the shape of the shingles and gives them the intended appearance. As a result, installation time would be nearly halved.

Product warranties, which are typically included with architectural shingles, have become useful marketing strategies for most manufacturers in enticing customers to buy their products.

These warranties will assist you in covering any repair or replacement costs if your roof develops a problem prematurely.

However, you should bear in mind that when getting architectural shingles, you should choose with the best brand not only because they have the best guarantee, but also because they are the highest quality in the industry.

Just because a product has a guarantee that states it will last for 50 years doesn't mean it will last that long.

Warranties are complicated and frequently include gaps, so don't expect to get a new roof for free.

Keep in mind that the expense of a new roof, no matter how low it may be, is still a significant investment.

Just because a product has a guarantee that states it will last for 50 years doesn't mean it will last that long.

Warranties are complicated and frequently include gaps, so don't expect to get a new roof for free.

Keep in mind that the expense of a new roof, no matter how low it may be, is still a significant investment.

Aluminum Roofing

Aluminum roofing is regarded for being one of the most affordable roofing materials on the market today.

Aluminum roofing is more typically used on commercial structures, but it is also projected to gain popularity among homeowners because it is an energy saver. Aluminum has a reputation for reflecting heat.

Some aluminum roof materials contain heat-saving chips, allowing you to save a significant amount of money on your energy expenses!

Aluminum roofing materials are more resistant to wind, hail, rain, fire, and rot than conventional roofing materials.

It can also help to prevent the quick growth of black mold, mildew, and algae, all of which can be harmful to one's health.

Roof and water leaks

Also, because aluminum roofing does not rust naturally, it does not require the costly paint processes to keep it from rusting.

Aluminum roofing comes in a variety of colors and designs, and it may be made to look like tiles.

The interlocking aluminum shingles have been created and engineered to make your life easier and your home maintenance–free for a long time.

Because aluminum roofing is essentially fireproof, your house insurance will likely decrease.

Roofing systems made of steel or aluminum are typically covered by a 50-year warranty. As a result, aluminum roofing is a wise investment for your business or home.

A few more dollars spent today will undoubtedly save you a lot of money in the future.

While looking for an effective roofing system, you should consider not only the appearance of your property, but also the protection it will provide and its long-term value.

Cedar Roofing

Wood shake is a roofing material that some homeowners prefer for a more aesthetically appealing finish on their homes, although it is not extensively employed by most homeowners or even in commercial applications.

Cedar shakes or shingles are made from a coniferous tree known for its natural qualities. Cedar roofing is a good choice for high-quality roofing in general.

Cedar is a beautiful and long-lasting wood with hues ranging from red to pale amber, and some with a honey-brown appearance. This type of cloth is a budget-friendly solution because of its endurance. It could also be a good choice for an outside structure.

To better comprehend the essence of cedar roofing, it is necessary to grasp how a cedar shingle or shake is created, as well as other fundamentals.

A cedar wood is first cut or slated, then trimmed and squared depending on whether it will be used for roofing or siding.

The width and thickness of a cedar shingle varies from 8 to 20 cm. Because the dimension of each cedar shingle varies, no two cedar shakes or shingles are identical.

Cedar roofing shakes are another name for cedar shingles.

After slating and molding each shingle to its proper size, the material is treated with chemicals or a Class B or C fire retardant to provide fire resistance.

Other chemical treatments are used to prevent moss, mildew, and fungal degradation, all of which are natural enemies of cedar roofing.

The slated shingles are kiln dried or put through a heating system process to make it a more acceptable roofing material.

The choice of a cedar roof not only contributes to the elegance and aesthetic of your home, but it also adds to its durability. The material becomes resistant to insects and moss or fungal development after being treated and kiln dried.

Because cedar roofing is a natural insulator, it keeps your home cool and comfortable in the summer and warm in the winter.

When you choose a cedar roof for your rooftop, you are not only enhancing the exterior aspects of your home, but you are also making a smart investment in the value of your property.

This is the only roofing material that not only has real and natural features, but also adds character to your home and may last for years if properly maintained.

Clay Tile Roofing

Clay tile roofing can be traced all the way back to China and the Middle East.

The use of the material was influenced and spread throughout Asia and Europe by these two regions.

Europeans have been utilizing clay tiles for roofs since the Middle Ages, and they introduced this roofing material to the United States in the 17th century.

Clay tile roofing has become well-known in the United States because to its durability, low maintenance, and heat resistance.

Clay tiles are distinguished primarily by their shape and content.

Resistance to breaking, absorption, resistance to freeze-thaw cycles, fireproof, and long lasting are some of its other characteristics. It can last for 50 to 70 years on average, but if the clay tile is of exceptional quality, it can last even longer.

This sort of material is well-known for its centuries-old traditional and architectural traits, which may be seen in historical relics of prominent structural towers and buildings.

Clay tiles for roofing are typically produced in two shapes: profile and flat. Pan and cover, S-tile, and interlocking profiles are the three types of profiles. Flat tiles come in two varieties: interlocking and non-interlocking.

Clay tile producers make a variety of quality tiles. Some tiles are of outstanding and long-lasting quality, while others are of poor quality and sold at a low price. The latter has a proclivity for corroding and wearing down over time.

This type of roofing material, unlike wood shakes and other roofing materials, does not require curing such as kiln drying or chemical treatment to increase its longevity. Because clay tile erodes over time, it's best used in dry locations where rainy seasons aren't predictable. Because clay tiles absorb a lot of water, it's important to think about where you're going to put them.

Since clay tile roofing is a big and heavy material, it requires a great deal of roof support.

Clay tiles do not need to be replaced if they leak or crack; instead, they can be mended.

Clay tiles are not only costly and labor-intensive, but they are also difficult to install. However, the use of the material gives your home or structure a particular appearance that no other roof can match.

When deciding on clay tile roofing, seek the opinion of a professional roofer or roofing consultant.

It's preferable to spend a greater price than to have to replace clay tile roofs every 5 or 6 years because you choose a low-quality clay tile roofing material.

Concrete Roofing

There are numerous developed roofing products available today that you may pick from to give your home an aesthetic appearance at a low cost, or a traditional appearance with the guarantee of a long-lasting on a sturdy framework.

Concrete roofing is a popular choice among homeowners these days because of the material's composition, which provides a solid foundation for your roof.

The cost or expense of employing concrete roofing may need to be considered. It's built to last, but you might have to pay a premium for it.

Concrete roofing is often connected with concrete tiles, which are a form of roofing material.

Concrete roofing is made out of cement-based materials such as concrete, fiber cement, minerals, and asphalt. Other types of concrete roofing include slate and composition shingles.

To make a thick and durable tile, concrete is molded under tremendous pressure. After installation, it is certain to last for at least sixty years, if not longer.

Concrete roofing is used on many European homes. Many of those properties have concrete roofs that are over a century old, which you may not be aware of. Concrete roofing is properly referred to be the roof of a lifetime for this reason.

Concrete roofing is the perfect option if you want to invest in your own property without having to worry about regular maintenance. It does not decay or become infested by insects. Moss may appear on the tiles, but it may be easily removed and cleaned.

It contributes to the beauty and artistic aspect of your home in addition to being a long-lasting material. Furthermore, the insulating effect it provides protects the interior of your home from heat, keeping you warm in the winter and pleasant or damp in the summer.

You were mistaken if you assumed concrete roofing consisted solely of the gray cement we see on a regular basis.

Innovative improvements have been developed over the years to redesign and recreate better and more exquisite concrete roofing tiles.

The traditional Spanish style ceramic roofing, which comes in a mission S-tile type, was once popular.

More options are available these days, ranging from Mediterranean style to shaking shingles in villa or flat tile types, as well as the classic cast stone and slate that looks as a flat tile type.

The Mission S-tile is so named because it resembles the letter "S," whereas the villa tiles resemble a double letter "S."

Flat tiles, on the other hand, are popular flat-surfaced materials that are designed to resemble wood shakes or slates.

Copper Roofing

Cooper is one of the world's oldest roofing materials. Copper has been prized for ages due to its exceptional long-term durability.

Copper is absolutely unique and gloriously gorgeous when it comes to the visual appeal it brings to a building, whether it's a house, a church, or a public place.

Copper may not have been as popular as aluminum and galvanized sheets in the previous two decades or so due to its high price, but only copper can provide that class that no other metal roofing can.

Copper has reclaimed its place as a preferred roofing material, particularly for individual residences. Copper is in high demand right now, as more and more people want copper roofing.

In comparison to other high-end roofing materials such as tiles, cedar, and slate, Bennington Copper Shingles roofs are fairly priced.

Because of their small weight, Bennington copper shingle roofs are simple to install. It's simple to care for and can last for up to 50 years.

The Revere Bennington ® roofing system boasts two key features: a manageable 4 ft copper shingle and concealed joint pans, making installation a breeze.

It has great weatherproofing and is simple to install. Copper nails, hip and ridge caps, and hip and ridge caps are all made to ASTM B370 standards, ensuring that the material will last a lifetime.

Copper sheet and other accessories, such as coil, are available in large quantities at Ryerson. It has a track record of producing high-quality roofing materials, particularly copper. It is, in fact, the largest provider of metal roofing materials in the United States.

Ryerson can easily deliver whatever sizes of copper sheets you require because they inspect their stocks on a regular basis.

Copper Accent Bay Window Roof Kit from Zappone, a reliable source of copper roofing material, is a new dimension in the copper roofing market. It's a complete copper roofing and accessory package.

Because of the simple instructions, even novices can mount the metals.

The kit is available in two sizes: a 6 feet bay and an 8 ft bay. If you want to try your hand at owning the timeless elegance of copper roofing, Zappone can help.

When it comes to styles and aesthetic qualities, copper roofing will never go out of style.

The antiquated effect of copper, on the other hand, makes it even more unique and difficult to imitate by any other metal roofing material on the market.

Corrugated Fiberglass Roofing

Corrugated fiberglass roofing is a highly recommended and cost-effective option to other roofing materials available on the market today in any given structure.

Installing a brand-new corrugated fiberglass roofing system in a commercial building is relatively simple, quick, and inexpensive.

Any business owner wants to get their business up and running as soon as possible, or at the very least avoid having their operations disrupted. Installing a metal roof is one of the efficient ways to accomplish such goals.

Sheet metal was the first corrugated roofing material to hit the market.

Stainless steel, fiberglass, aluminum, painted steel, and coated steel are just a few of the materials accessible nowadays.

Corrugated roofs are typically coated with a specific finish that prevents corrosion and rust. For many years, these attributes made it a popular roofing option among commercial building owners.

Among the corrugated roof installations, the fiberglass corrugated roofing system is one of the most intriguing.

Many people appreciate the fact that corrugated fiberglass roofing can be translucent, allowing for natural lighting while also lowering their energy bills.

Fiberglass is also impermeable and extremely durable, while also being significantly lower in weight.

Another distinguishing trait is its capacity to give greater stiffness than a flat metal sheet of similar thickness and weight.

As a result, the cost and weight of the built roof can be significantly reduced.

It's vital to remember, though, that if you're thinking about installing corrugated fiberglass roofing, you'll need to select the correct roofing contractor.

Roofing professionals with vast experience erecting roofs, particularly metal or corrugated fiberglass roofing, are plentiful.

Most experienced veteran contractors have plenty of experience with metal or fiberglass roofs and can do thorough regular roof inspections if necessary.

If you're considering new roofing or even roofing repairs, make sure to check out your contractor's references. It's also crucial to insist on a signed contract before signing a contract with any roofing firm.

The contract should specify the sort of roofing material used, as well as the timeline and estimated completion date, as well as the agreed-upon price.

You will be able to avoid complications during the installation of your new roof in this way.

Elastomeric Roofing

Rubber roofing, also known as elastomeric roofing, is a form of synthetic roofing material that is made up of recycled rubber.

This rubber is chipped off at the rubber mill, and the small pieces are blended with various chemicals to make RRPV (Recycled Rubber Polyurethane Elastomer) or EPDM (Elastomeric Polyurethane Elastomer) (Ethylene Propylene Diene Monomer).

Rubber roof manufacturers frequently add powdered stone, limestone, or slate to the composition to achieve UV filtering capability. It also improves the material's appearance and durability.

An underlayment is required for the installation of elastomeric roofing. Roofers should have finished putting the membrane roofing underlayment before the construction work is left for the day.

The rationale for this is to keep water out of the framework when it rains suddenly, as this will wet the plywood and insulating board within.

And if this happens without your knowledge, there's a good chance that moisture on the insulation board or plywood would cause the material to be readily destroyed sooner or later.

Elastomeric roofing can be applied with liquid elastomeric coatings and protective membranes that look like rubber.

It may function as a maintenance and protection for the rubber roof during the construction process to prevent leakage or ripping down.

Rubber coating not only fixes unpleasant leaks, but it also saves money because to its heat reflectivity. However, correct coating selection is required, as not all elastomeric coatings are created equal.

They may differ in terms of tensile strength and elongation, as well as in terms of durability and stickiness.

Your roofing specialist will be able to provide you with the right guidance on this.

Because of its anti-porous property, elastomeric roofing is completely watertight as compared to clay tile roofing.

It's also fire-proof and all that's required is a single-ply coating. The material can withstand ultraviolet light, gases, and even snow and ice because of its UV filtering capacity. Depending on the rubber's durability, this sort of roofing material can last up to 40 years.

Do not use this sort of roofing material if you reside in an area where temperatures can drop to as low as 20 degrees Celsius.

In cold conditions, elastomeric roofs are not very flexible.

PVC Roofing System

PVC roof sheets are one of the most technologically advanced roofing materials.

PVC roofing materials are used by both industrial and residential constructions all over the world because of their durability and functionality.

PVC roofing materials are used on most sporting stadiums across the world, from the Wimbledon tennis courts in England to the ice sports arena on the Munich Olympic Ground.

The endurance of the PVC roofing system is a major factor for modern architects.

The Stade de France in Paris is one of the first notable examples of PVC roofing. The 60,000-square-meter roof was constructed in preparation for the 1998 World Cup.

The PVC materials are resistant to a wide range of weather conditions, including hail, thunderstorms, and hurricanes, which tend to hit the United States on a frequent basis.

To relieve yourself of constant stress, your roof materials should be able to withstand the wrath of nature.

PVC roofing materials are practically fireproof as well.

This is a vital factor to consider when it comes to protecting not only your goods, but also the lives of the people who dwell in any structure.

PVC roofing materials are also corrosion resistant, making them almost maintenance free for an extended period of time. PVC membrane's reflecting surface can help lower a building's cooling requirements. Such a feature would only cut your energy usage costs.

This roofing technique is slightly less expensive than other roofing materials currently on the market.

Its popularity for outdoor use is boosted by the fact that it is both affordable and lightweight.

PVC roofing sheets also have the longest track record in terms of application. As a result, you may rest certain that professionals have rigorously verified the quality and durability of PVC materials over time.

The U.S. Environmental Protection Agency has categorized the roofing system, along with TPO or thermoplastic polyolefin, as roofing products that can reduce energy consumption and concerns linked with heat build-up, smog, and air pollution.

Poly Foam Roofing

It's possible that having a roof made of poly foam material does not appeal to you.

The truth is that poly foam roofing is only popular in hot climatic areas of the United States, such as California.

Homeowners in the arid region, particularly those with flat roofs, would undoubtedly appreciate the advantages of poly foam roofing.

Sealants, adhesives, and other synthetic-based materials are all composed of polyurethane foam, which is a substance made of any polymer. Your primary roofing material is not poly foam.

Regardless of the type, it truly complements the present one. Its primary function is to insulate the roof substrate so that heat is not trapped.

Although poly foam is quite expensive to install since it requires a professional, there are companies that specialize in poly foam roofing installation.

If you're sold on the concept, you'll want to be especially cautious when hiring an installer. Check to see if the contractor has a solid reputation. If necessary, look for referrals.

There are roofing companies that provide a cost-effective poly foam installation.

Check to see if it can handle a polyurethane foam roofing system. It has a track record of success, which is essential for roofing contractors.

Make sure their employees are well-trained in this area so you can trust them. You may rest comfortable that what you have is thermally resistant, seamless, light, and long-lasting.

Poly foam is simple to keep clean because it is so compact that leakage is impossible.

Elastomeric coatings can be put to the area to repair the material if there are any leaks.

Better yet, seek assistance from the contractor that installed your foam so that it is properly cared for. Inquire if maintenance is included in the deal; if it is, you will be able to save even more money.

The only disadvantage is that if the foam is left out in the sun, it will degrade. The sun's heat dries out the foam, causing it to shatter into fragments.

To prevent the foam from drying out, a substantial amount of coating is required first.
The pros recommend acrylic latex coating since it is inexpensive and simple to apply, and

it can be purchased off the shelf at your local store.

If you need to invest in foam roofing, you can get firsthand information from people you know in your neighborhood. If it is worthwhile to pay the money, you can gather more suggestions and have better selections.

Nothing beats being cautious when it comes to spending money on foam roofing; after all, a solid investment in poly foam roofing is a good way to safeguard your home.

Patio Roofing

Why not extend your living space outside if you have some spare room in your garden that you want to make the most of?

It would be nice to sit outside and sip cool lemonades while watching the flowers bloom in the privacy of your own lawn every now and again.

Patios are a terrific home addition for dining and recreation for family and friends instead of keeping confined in the enclosed quarters of your home.

From simple Sunday barbeques to elegant dinner parties, a well-designed patio can accommodate every occasion.

There are many different patio designs to pick from, and you can customize them to fit your needs and preferences.

However, choosing a nice patio roofing to complement your home and offer you with the necessary shelter for your outdoor enjoyment is important.

The prospect can be intimidating, but here are some helpful hints for selecting the best patio roofing for your property.

Patio canopies are frequently made of polycarbonate sheets. The material enables some light to get through while blocking UV rays and rain effectively.

Most polycarbonate roofing comes with a 10-year fade and crack resistance warranty.

Canvas awnings are another choice for your patio roofing, and they come in a variety of shapes and colors to pick from.

You can even add a freestanding metal frame with a rollaway fabric awning to relocate your temporary patio around your yard.

For all types of weather, aluminum patio roofing may give a more substantial and long-lasting protection.

For many years, aluminum patio roofing materials can endure rust, chipping, peeling, and cracking.

The lattice form of patio roofing is also an option if you desire a light, airy vibe. Lattice is available in natural wood tones to fit your home's existing color scheme. Lattice roofing can provide some shade without obstructing too much light.

However, if you want to get the most out of your patio roofing, you should blend lattice and solid roofing.

You may feel safe leaving your patio equipment under a strong roof all year while still benefiting from the well-ventilated effect provided by the lattice roofing.

These are just alternative that you can look up for your patio roofs.

Your decision will largely be based on what is most important to you and what best suits your needs and lifestyle.

Tin Roofing

Tin roofing has been used for millennia. Its popularity has never dwindled, owing to the fact that it is the most cost-effective roofing material.

The material is also lightweight, long-lasting, corrosion-resistant, and has remarkable forming capabilities. It also absorbs heat quickly, allowing it to melt snow and prevent ice damming.

Tin is a cost-effective weatherproofing material.

Tin roofing, as opposed to other metal roofing materials such as lead, copper, aluminum, zinc, and galvanized iron, or alternative roofing materials such as rubber and cedar shake, is an ideal choice for individuals on a budget.

Tin roofing is simple to install, and it requires little upkeep. It is the most widely utilized material in the United States' mass housing program.

Tin roofing has a similar lifespan to other metal roofing materials.

The collection of dirt and discoloration on tin roofing is a regular problem that homeowners face.

If not addressed immediately, this will cause damage to the roof over time. Corrosion signs may begin to show on roof surfaces.

During the tin roof construction, if several perforated portions were left open, these holes will leak if it rains. The leaks should be addressed as soon as they are discovered.

Leaking roofs are widespread in valleys, roof-to-wall connections, and slope steepness.

These areas of the roof should be thoroughly examined for unattractive stains and filth, as well as potential leaks.

Coatings can help to repair any damage that rust may cause to your roof. Similarly, sealants can aid in preventing water from seeping via leaks.

There are numerous sealants and coatings on the market. Electrometric coating substance is widely used by homeowners.

Painting your roof will enhance its beauty and add a touch of luxury to it. Paint should not be mistaken for a coating substance, even if it may serve that role for a short time.

Paint conceals unattractive sealant and coating areas. It also provides old-looking roofs a new look. A well-painted roof is a roof that has been well-maintained.

Tin roofing is simple to clean, even with just water. Strong chemicals are no longer required, particularly if the roofs are brand new.

Roof washing should be done on a regular basis to avoid the accumulation of dirt, which can harbor microorganisms that can ruin the roof.

If there is obstinate dirt, moderate chemicals should be used to protect the color of the paint and avoid chipping.

Tin roofing is very economical and long-lasting, allowing you to save more money. You may also get your money's worth if you take good care of your roof.

Commercial Roofing

Small and large-scale enterprises alike desire a roofing firm that can perform commercial roofing services while not interfering with their usual business activities.

Several roofing companies offer specialized services for commercial premises, such as clearing trash from parking lots and clearing entryways of any obstacles so that your business may continue to operate normally.

For your business building, you can select from a variety of roofing materials. The cost, slope of your roof, and weather conditions in your area will all play a role in your decision.

Asphalt shingles are the most common form of shingle used on both residential and commercial roofing constructions.

Asphalt shingles can last for 2-3 decades if reinforced with wood fibers, fiberglass, or organic compounds.

Laminated shingles are similarly constructed of asphalt, but they come in a larger range of colors and textures that give the appearance of more expensive shake or slate tiles.

Steel, Standing Seam, Copper, and Metal Tie are some of the metal goods used in commercial roofing materials today.

Metal roofing is predicted to last between 30 and 50 years if correctly placed and is substantially less expensive than asphalt shingles.

This sort of roofing material can endure most adverse weather conditions, but it has been known to dent over time.

Copper is another option to explore, but it is significantly more expensive than aluminum. Copper roofs, on the other hand, can last up to 100 years.

When it comes to wood shakes, especially for commercial roofing, cedar is the clear winner. The typical cost of wood shake application might be up to 50% greater than that of other roofing systems.

Slate shingles are significantly heavier and more difficult to install. They are also fairly delicate, but they may bring beauty and elegance to any structure.

Tiles are another option for your business roofing needs. Typically, tiles are constructed of clay, rubber, or concrete.

Clay tiles are more expensive than concrete tiles, but they function and last about the same. Because tiles are much heavier than other roofing materials, you may require additional structural support for your roof.

So, whether you're constructing a new project or repairing your existing business roofing, it's critical to use a qualified roofing contractor who can do the job well.

Roofing Disasters And How To Avoid Them

Your home's roof is the first line of defense against natural elements such as high winds, heavy rain, sleet, and snow.

Conducting a thorough inspection of each spring-inside and out-can help you avoid costly problems later on. Look for the following warning signs that your roof is not sufficiently protecting your home:

A home inspection should begin with a search for attic leaks. This can happen and is most noticeable after large, driving rains. Inspect the walls and ceilings in each room of the house as well.

Ceiling stains are another clue that your roof needs to be repaired. Peeling interior or exterior paint or wallpaper, which can occur as a result of excessive moisture or high humidity, can also be an indication of poor attic ventilation.

If extra ventilation is required, it can be reasonably simple and affordable to install—even if a new roof is not required.

Cracks in flashing around chimneys and vents, as well as worn-out, rotting, or missing shingles, are the most prevalent outside leak sources. Examine your gutters for debris, such as granules in the gutter. If you detect an excessive amount of granules, it could be a sign of aging shingles that need to be replaced.

While you're up there, look for missing, broken, or curled shingles. These should be replaced as soon as possible in order to avoid structural damage to your roof deck and the interior of your home. If any shingles are blistered, decaying, or appear "dirty," they must be replaced as well.

If you discover any of these potential issues and are in need of repairs, the first and most crucial step is to choose a reputable roofing contractor.

According to GAF Materials Corporation, North America's largest roofing producer, poorly installed or designed roofing systems cost American households billions of dollars each year.

Fortunately, most concerns can be avoided with a professionally installed, maintained, and/or repaired roofing system.

GAF provides access to a database of prequalified, factory-certified roofing contractors. Every contractor is licensed and insured, and they all promise to treat the homeowner's roof as if it were their own.

Roofing Insurance Considerations

You should have no illusions about the dangers of roofing.

Working at such heights, and often in some rather harsh conditions, exposes workers to danger on a regular basis.

If a company is judged liable for any injuries or accidents that occur on the job, they may be required to pay out substantial sums of money out of their own pockets if they do not have worker's compensation insurance. Small roofing companies may face financial devastation as a result of this.

Roofing insurance is not cheap, but it is far less expensive than not having it if you need it.

Types of roofing insurance

There are two types of articles that you should think about employing to protect yourself from accidents or injury.

Workers compensation insurance protects against workplace injuries, whereas public liability insurance protects against comparable events involving members of the public or third-party property.

Workers compensation insurance

Workers compensation insurance is one of the two forms of roofing insurance that you should seriously consider purchasing because you are in grave danger of having to pay hefty settlements out of your own pocket if you do not have it.

If the worst happens and one of your employees is killed in a workplace accident, this value can go into the hundreds of thousands of dollars.

Having workers compensation insurance is the only way to avoid this.

Public liability insurance

Anyone who need public liability insurance, from cat sitters to roofers, can obtain it.

In terms of roofing insurance, this is yet another essential product for your company.

If a member of the public wanders into a piece of scaffolding or a shingle you just installed falls off the roof and smashes a car, you are liable for the damages as well as the cost of any necessary repairs.

In some situations, this can amount to a substantial sum of money. In comparison, the monthly premium you will be required to pay is negligible.

Bring down the cost of your roofing insurance

If you're concerned about the cost of roofing insurance, you might want to consider joining a buying group of some kind.

If you are already a member of a trade association, you may discover that they have negotiated good prices on all elements of roofing insurance, and taking advantage of these deals can save you a significant amount of time and money.

Buyers should inquire about a company's roofing insurance.

If you are a consumer seeking to install a new roof, you should always check with any possible roofing business to see what kind of roofing insurance they offer.

Because the cost of roofing insurance may be fairly significant, some roofing companies have recently opted to purchase a general contractor's insurance policy.

If the roofing company you hire causes any inadvertent damage to your home or anything in or around it, you will only be compensated if they carry roofing insurance.

Roofing insurance companies will pay out faster and more easily than you would if you had to rely on the roofing company to repay you.

Roofing Shingle Warranties

The Basic Warranty

Whatever roofing shingles you choose, they should meet regulatory standards and come with a minimum warranty that the shingle will operate as expected.

The typical guarantee period is 15 to 40 years, however a growing number of shingles come with a lifetime warranty.

While most roofing shingle warranties are considered standard, there can be considerable variances in warranty coverage amongst shingles that are otherwise comparable.

Perhaps most crucially, some warranties only cover the cost of the shingles, not the labor required to remove and replace the old roof.

It's worth noting that most shingle manufacturers include detailed installation instructions, which I've included below.

Wind Warranty

Shingles can be severely damaged by high winds. Winds that are strong enough to break the shingles off your roof will do it, but even lesser winds can inflict significant damage.

In high enough winds, shingles will lift, even if only for a second. This could be the beginning of two issues.

First, debris and moisture can blow in under the shingle when it rises. The dirt and moisture are trapped once the shingle returns to its original location. If there is too much moisture in your home, it may leak through the roof and cause damage. The trapped debris also prevents the tile from resting flat, allowing more moisture and dirt to enter.

Wind also causes shingles to distort, allowing additional moisture and debris to enter the home.

Algae Resistant Warranty

Algae development is a typical roofing issue that results in dark streaks on the tiles. Although the algae can be removed, it will most certainly reappear, particularly if you live in a humid region.

If you've experienced algae issues in the past, your shingle warranty should include algae-resistant coverage.

Roofing Q&A: New Roof And Re-Roofing Answers

1. How do I know if I need a new roof?

The roof should be inspected on a regular basis. You should keep an eye on it. The indications that you might require a new roof are as follows.

· Your roof is between twenty and twenty-five years old.
· The shingles are excessively cracking, curling, or they are blistering.
· There are many shingles that are missing and/are torn or damaged.
· The roof is leaking in many places.

2. How much does a new roof cost?

There's no way to know how much a new roof will set you back. Before an estimate can be made, several factors must be considered. A price quotation or estimate could be made based on the information.

Some of the considerations are:

· Size of roof
· Materials to be used

· Location of house (this is needed to determine which materials would be best for that area's weather)
  · Is it for a new house or a re-roofing
  · State costs and taxes
  · Type of home

After that, you can have several contractors bid on the project to get the best price.

3. When re-roofing, should I peel off old layers or simply add a new layer of shingles?

It is suggested that you replace the shingles on your roof. Scraping the old layers will take more time and energy, and the thickness of the shingles will be reduced as a result of the peeling, perhaps resulting in future leaks. It covers the inner section of the roof and gives relief from further leaks by putting fresh layers of shingles to your roof. Obviously, it would be far less expensive.

4. What kinds of questions should I ask a roofing contractor?

Getting a roof contractor to work on your roof requires some assurance and clarity. You might ask the contractor the following questions to clear up any worries you have about his or her services:

• Ask about your roofing contractor's reputation in his or her field of expertise. It will reveal whether they are indeed providing exceptional service to their customers.

• Ask about their business operations. This involves determining whether they have the proper licenses to operate such a business, as well as whether they are insured in case of unforeseen events that may occur during installation.

• Finally, ask about the actual roofing construction as well as post-construction services and warranties. Determine whether they can describe how they will create your roofing in layman's words, what materials will be utilized, and what services and warranties they offer in the event of leaks or damage to your roof within a certain period following construction.

5. What kinds of questions should I ask references of a roofing contractor?

When you are unfamiliar with a certain type of business, you may request referrals from people who are familiar with the work of the roofing contractor you are investigating.

From references, ask about the roofing contractor, particularly from clients who have had work done by him. You might ask your roofing contractor references questions like the ones below:

• First, ask about their relationship with the contractor. Perhaps the contractor is a relative or friend of one of your references. This will offer you an indication of how well that reference is acquainted with the contractor.

• You can question as to whether they have hired a roofing contractor. Inquire if they were present during the roof's construction, while also allowing your reference to speak about the service's quality.

• Finally, inquire about the service's reliability, as well as whether it can survive the various outdoor conditions that surround the roof. You will have no doubts about the contractor's integrity because the reference will tell you everything.

About The Author

AnThony Legins is a real estate coach and mentor with a passion to show you how to become successful in real estate investing.

He is a licensed builder, licensed real estate broker, developer, investor, and consultant who has been active in real estate since 2004. He is experienced in residential and commercial real estate and creative real estate financing.

Host of "How To Buy The Hood" and "The Armond & AnThony Show" on REH TV - Real Estate Heat TV - The Hottest New Real Estate Channel and podcast. Also now airing on 4Biddenknowledge.tv

He is a best-selling author and a prolific blogger with followings on several high-profile blog sites including Medium, Entrepreneurs Handbook, Better Marketing, 4Biddenknowledge and more.

Visit http://www.313builders.com today!

Other Books By AnThony Legins

- The Ultimate Painting & Wallpapering Guide (Best Seller)
- The Ultimate Kitchen Remodeling & Renovation Guide (Best Seller)
- The Unconventional Guide To Recycling (Best Seller)
- Detroit Real Estate Investors Handbook
- Investing In Real Estate With Little or No Money Down
- Investing In Commercial Real Estate
- Learn The Lingo – The Ultimate Real Estate Vocabulary Guide
- The Small Business Survival Guide

Made in United States
Troutdale, OR
09/29/2024

23204916R00056